EXPLORING CAVES

Jill Bryant

Contents

What Is a Cave?

A cave is an open, hollow space in the ground, that is naturally formed. Most caves are big enough for at least one person to crawl inside. Caves can take millions of years to form. They are usually formed out of rock, but some caves are under ice. Other caves are under water. Most caves are hidden from view.

The opening of a cave is called the "mouth".

The shape of a large cave is described as a cavern. A cavern is big enough to stand up in. It might be the size of a small living room in a house, or as large as a huge aircraft hangar.

Many caves have long, winding tunnels and narrow passages. This is known as a cave system. People often enjoy exploring caves.

Different Types of Caves

Caves can be found in many environments. The most common types of caves are limestone caves, sea caves, glacier caves and lava tubes. These caves are all around the world.

Limestone Caves

Most caves are formed out of a type of soft rock called limestone. Limestone is made from the crushed shells of sea animals. It contains a **mineral** called **calcium**.

When it rains, water dribbles along the surface of the limestone rock and seeps into cracks in its surface. The water **dissolves** the calcium and makes the cracks grow larger and larger. After millions of years, caves form out of these large cracks.

This cave has been formed out of limestone rock.

Sea Caves

Sea caves are formed along coastlines by big, crashing waves. The force of the waves hits the rocky cliffs on the shore, over and over, and eventually, caves appear. As time passes, powerful surf can break apart the roof of a sea cave. This leaves an open hole. Sometimes, the force of the waves makes water blast up into the air through the hole.

Think and Talk About ...

Cave diving is a sport that involves diving underwater in caves, with special breathing equipment. People must pass a special course before doing this high-risk activity.

During low tide, people can explore many sea caves safely.

Glacier Caves

Glacier caves are formed out of ice. When ice in a glacier melts, small amounts of water flow along the frozen surface into cracks and **crevasses**, and begin to carve tiny openings. When rivers gush over the ice, the spaces underneath the glaciers grow into large caves, passages and tunnels.

When sunshine hits the opening of this glacier cave in Norway, the ice looks blue.

Think and Talk About ...

Around the world, the temperature is rising and more ice is melting. If enough melting occurs, the roofs of glacier caves will collapse and the caves will disappear.

Lava Tubes

Some caves are formed from the lava of volcanoes. After a volcano erupts, the hot lava flows down the volcano, forming **molten** rivers. The top layer cools and hardens into rock. The lava underneath the crusty top layer is still hot liquid, and when this liquid centre drains away, a hard, hollow shell, called a "lava tube", is left behind.

One of the Undara lava tubes in Far North Queensland, Australia, is so long that it takes more than 15 minutes to walk from one end to the other.

Stalactites and Stalagmites

After a limestone cave has been formed, water and air can affect how the cave looks inside. Water, filled with minerals, drips into a cave through the ceiling. The water then **evaporates**, leaving behind small amounts of the mineral. More water slowly drips down from the ceiling of the cave, forming a hollow tube, known as a "soda straw". Thousands of years later, the tube fills with crusty minerals. It grows longer and thicker. These icicle-shaped features hanging down from the ceiling of the cave are called "stalactites".

Droplets of water from the top of a cave form stalactites.

Stalagmites rise from the bottom of the cave floor.

When water dripping into the cave splashes onto the cave floor, it slowly creates another feature. These upward-pointing spikes are called "stalagmites". Sometimes, stalactites and stalagmites join together and make a column.

Mineral deposits from water can grow in other formations inside a cave, too. Some of these are named after the way they look, for example, tables, curtains and drapery. Rock flowers and frostwork can form when crystals from minerals grow in complex patterns.

This cave mineral deposit is called "drapery", because it looks like drapes (or curtains).

Minerals in caves can create patterns called "gypsum flowers".

Think and Talk About ...

Stalactites and stalagmites form in glacier caves, too. Instead of being made from minerals, they are made from ice.

Cave Explorers

Cavers

There are two different types of people who explore caves. People who explore caves for fun, adventure or exercise are known as cavers, or **spelunkers**. These people usually visit well-known caves that are easy to find and not too difficult to explore. They enjoy crawling through narrow spaces and following paths in the dark.

Think and Talk About ...

The word "spelunker" comes from the ancient Greek word for "cave".

Cave Scientists

Scientists also explore caves, to study and research their features. Cave scientists are known as speleologists. They explore many different types of caves to take photos, collect samples and gather data.

Both cavers and speleologists need to be very careful when exploring caves, because there are risks of getting stuck, falling or becoming lost. They wear protective clothing and carry safety equipment at all times.

A speleologist studies the environment inside a cave.

Many other types of scientists visit caves to carry out research and collect samples. Biologists study plant and animal life inside caves. Every year, they find new underground species. Photographs make a lasting record of the animals they discover. Scientists who study prehistoric people sift through sand to find bones, tools and coins. By examining objects found in caves, they learn about the past.

Some scientists study the climate inside caves. They record the temperature, the amount of moisture and the movement of air. Scientists help to protect caves that are visited by many people.

A biologist studies a bat inside a cave.

Soil experts study **bacteria** from underground soil samples. This bacteria could be used to make new medicines. Caves may hold a cure for serious illnesses. Scientists can learn a lot from caves.

Climate scientists use this device (called an "ultrasonic anemometer") to measure the speed and direction of moving air in a cave.

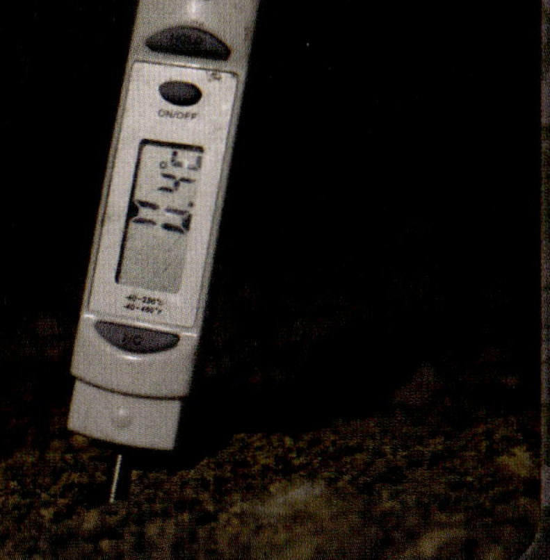

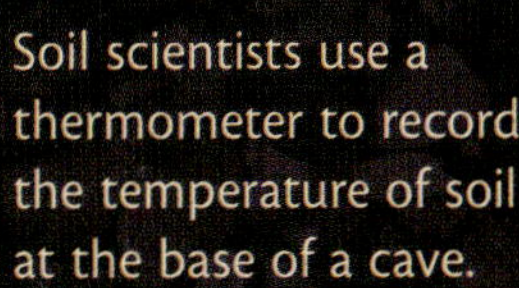

Soil scientists use a thermometer to record the temperature of soil at the base of a cave.

Caving Equipment

Exploring caves can be a dangerous activity. People who go inside caves need to be aware of falling rocks, low ceilings and unexpected drops in the floor of the cave. Some caves contain underground streams and slippery rocks. Crystals on the walls of caves can be very sharp. Cave explorers learn to watch for **hazards** and avoid them.

Before leaving home, cave explorers must plan their route carefully. They tell someone where they are going and when they expect to return. They wear protective clothing, helmets with a light and sturdy shoes. Each person should carry a large bottle of water and some snacks. Water and snacks can be important for survival if explorers have to stay underground longer than expected.

Think and Talk About ...

If a person exploring a cave gets a headache or has trouble breathing, this is often a sign that the air is not good. All explorers should exit the cave as quickly as possible.

Cave Exploring Equipment

To be safe in a cave, people should have the following safety equipment:

Caves around the World

Booming Ice Chasm, Canada

A cave known as the Booming Ice Chasm, is found high in the icy cliffs of the Rocky Mountains, in Canada. It is made of frozen limestone, and explorers use pickaxes to chip into the ice and make toeholds. When a chunk of ice falls, the noise echoes through the chilly cavern.

Booming Ice Chasm

Cave of the Crystals, Mexico

The Cave of the Crystals, a limestone cave in Mexico, was discovered by miners 300 metres under the ground, in 2000. It is extremely hot in this cave, with very high humidity, so explorers cannot spend very long in the cave at one time. This cave contains some of the largest crystals ever found – some up to 12 metres in length, the size of telephone poles!

Cave of the Crystals

Mammoth Cave, United States of America

Mammoth Cave

The longest cave system in the world, Mammoth Cave, is in Kentucky, the USA, beneath gently rolling hills. It contains more than 640 kilometres of known caverns and passageways. Many thrill-seeking visitors come to visit and explore this impressive cave system. Mammoth Cave is classed as a World Heritage site, to help **preserve** the caves.

Wookey Hole Caves, England

Wookey Hole Caves

The Wookey Hole Caves, in England, are limestone caves with a river running through them. The discovery of ancient tools reveals that people lived in these caves about 45 000 years ago. Many people explore these caves by cave diving – swimming through the parts of the cave that are under water, using special breathing equipment. The temperature in the caves remains steady at 11 °C and the air is moist. These conditions are ideal for making cheese. Today, cheddar cheese is aged in the caves and sold to grocery stores and to people who visit this popular site.

Dragon's Breath Cave, Namibia

Beneath the Kalahari Desert in Namibia, Africa, lies a cave that has a massive underground lake. This lake is the largest in the world – except for lakes under glaciers. Cave diving is popular in the crystal-clear water. A rare fish species, the Golden Cave Catfish, lives in this lake.

There are only 150 Golden Cave Catfish in the world, and all of them live in the lake in Dragon's Breath Cave.

Kungur Ice Cave, Russia

Fifty caves and seventy lakes make up the underground world of rock and ice known as the Kungur Ice Cave, in Russia. Ice-crystal shapes and stalagmites decorate the rock surfaces. The temperature remains below zero, even when the outside temperature is as high as 35 °C. This cave is a very popular tourist destination.

Kungur Ice Cave

Dongzhong Cave, China

A cave can provide shelter, safety and learning. For 27 years, students from Mao village in China went to classes, sang in a choir and played basketball – in a cave! Mid-Cave Primary School, deep inside the Dongzhong Cave, closed in 2011. Resources and education opportunities are limited in this area, so children are hoping for a new school soon.

Mid-Cave Primary School in Dongzhong Cave

Yarrangobilly Caves, Australia

The Yarrangobilly Caves, a group of five caves near the Snowy Mountains in New South Wales, Australia, were formed inside deep gorges. Stalagmites, stalactites, cave coral – a small, bubble-shaped cave decoration – and other features fill huge caverns, which people can explore through stairs, ramps and paths. The limestone rock of these caves is 440 million years old.

Stalactites hang from the ceiling of the Yarrangobilly Caves.

The Deepest Cave on Earth: Krubera Cave

Krubera Cave is located high in a limestone mountain, not far from the Black Sea, in the country of Georgia, at the border of Europe and Asia. Above ground, the land is covered in dense forest. A small opening in the rock marks the cave's entrance.

Krubera Cave is located in the northwestern part of Georgia.

With a recorded depth of 2197 metres, Krubera Cave is the deepest explored cave on Earth. Explorers compare descending into the depths of this cave to climbing Mount Everest! The entire cave system is 16 058 metres long. It splits into two branches at 200 metres and divides into many more twisting paths at 1300 metres.

A caver prepares to enter the mouth of Krubera Cave.

Krubera Cave is best known for its deep wells. The longest well is 152 metres. The cave also contains many water-blocked passages, known as "sumps". Other features include narrow passages, cave **decorations**, high waterfalls and icy-cold lakes.

Temperatures in the cave range from 0.5 °C to 5 °C. Even though it is very cold, beetles, spiders, scorpions and shrimps can survive in the cave. It is also home to four new species of eyeless insects, called springtails, that creep close to the bottom of the cave.

Krubera Cave is a popular site for cavers, scientists and people who are curious about exploring under the ground.

A caver descends into Krubera Cave using lights and safety equipment.

The springtail insect lives on the dark cave floor.

Cave Art

Ancient Paintings

Cave art is paintings on cave walls and ceilings. Ancient cave art can be found in caves all over the world. Some people believe that cave art was created in prehistoric times as a way for people to communicate stories.

The first cave paintings were discovered in the Altamira Cave in northern Spain, in 1880. The paintings of animals and symbols in this cave are thought to be as old as 24 000 years – among the oldest cave paintings in the world. People used ochre, a natural mineral found in the ground, for the paint, with colours ranging from red to brown, yellow and black.

Bison are painted on the ceiling of the Altamira Cave. The use of colour, shading, and point of view show great artistic skill.

The Lascaux Caves in southern France are famous for their large paintings of horses. There are also pictures of bulls, cows, deer, ibex (a species of wild goat) and bears. There are nearly 2000 pictures decorating the walls and ceilings of these caves. The artwork is thought to be about 19 000 years old. The entrance to the Lascaux Caves was blocked off for many years, which helped to keep the paintings safe and well preserved. Ancient artwork is usually found in dry caves. Too much moisture would make the paintings wash away.

Discovered in the 1940s, the cave art in the Lascaux Caves provides clues about human history.

Think and Talk About ...

Four boys and their dog discovered the Lascaux Caves on 12 September, 1940.

Handprint Outlines

Scientists have discovered that some cave artists used hollow animal bones to blow paint onto cave walls to outline shapes, such as their hands. Painters would place one hand on the rock and then blow paint through a bone pipe over and around their hand. In this way, they created the outline of a handprint. The entrance to Cave of the Hands in Patagonia, Argentina, is covered in red, purple, yellow and black **silhouettes** of hands. The paintings are thought to be around 10 000 years old.

Ancient hand prints are still visible in the Cave of the Hands, Argentina.

Handprint outlines also appear in limestone caves in Indonesia. The hand paintings in a cave in Sulawesi are believed to be about 40 000 years old, which are the oldest cave hand paintings in the world.

Cave art discoveries such as these show that humans were painting in caves in all different parts of the world at the same time. Studying cave art helps us to understand what life was like for the people who made the art, long ago.

Think and Talk About ...

Africa has more cave art than the six other continents on Earth. The Cave of Swimmers in Egypt includes 10 000-year-old paintings of human figures who look like they are swimming.

Cave Treasures

Sometimes, treasures are discovered in caves. There are many stories describing findings of **caches** of precious coins and jewels in caves around the world. Treasure-seekers can look for years and not find anything, and sometimes people stumble upon rare treasures completely by accident.

Beads

Among the oldest treasures found in caves are ancient beads. Forty-one snail shells pierced with holes were found in the Blombos Cave in South Africa, in 2004. Scientists believe humans drilled holes in these shells with a bone tool and used them for jewellery. The beads are around 75 000 years old and have flecks of red paint on them. There were layers of sand protecting the beads when they were discovered.

The discovery of beads made from snail shells led scientists to believe that humans were able to use symbols at least 75 000 years ago.

Crowns and Coins

One of the biggest cave treasures was found in a cave located on a cliff in the desert, near the Dead Sea, in Israel. Hidden for more than 5500 years in the Cave of the Treasures was a **hoard** of 429 **artefacts**, including objects made from copper, stone and ivory. Ten crowns, with animal decorations, were among the treasures.

In 2014, 26 gold and silver coins were discovered in a cave in Dovedale, England. They are thought to be from Roman times and the Late Iron Age.

This crown was discovered in 1961 inside the Cave of the Treasures, Israel.

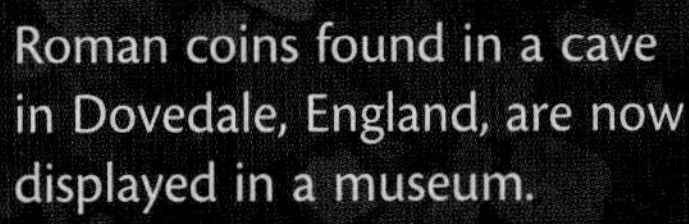

Roman coins found in a cave in Dovedale, England, are now displayed in a museum.

Underground Creatures

Many animals live inside caves. They have adapted to live in near-dark and pitch-black environments. When the weather outside is windy or wet, or when they are looking for a place to sleep or eat, animals can slip inside the entrances of caves. These creatures include snakes, mice, rats, birds, raccoons and bears.

Raccoons sometimes enter caves to sleep or eat.

Think and Talk About ...

Troglobites, or animals that live in caves, live ten times longer than above-ground animals. Cave bats, for example, often live to be 20 or 30 years old.

In the **twilight** zone, where there is some light in a cave, but not much, salamanders, spiders, moths, millipedes, crickets, frogs and bats are comfortable. Cave bats' waste – or guano – is rich with nutrients that are important to the survival of other cave animals.

In the dark zone inside a cave, where no light reaches, the animals have adapted to the complete darkness. They are usually blind and colourless, and they never go outside. Fish, worms and spiders live in this zone. Some dark-zone creatures, such as springtails, have long antennae – their main organ for sensing. In the Waitomo Caves in New Zealand, glow-worms give off a blue light from their tails.

The Texas blind salamander lives in a pool in a cave in Texas, the USA.

The largest species of cave-dwelling bat is the endangered Bulmer's fruit bat, from Papua New Guinea. Adult females have a wingspan of up to 1 metre.

Living in Caves

Many people think that humans used to live in caves. But no one knows for sure. Human bones, tools, bits of clothing and firepits have been found in caves.

Lots of scientists think that early humans preferred living in rock shelters. Compared to caves, rock shelters had natural light and fresh air. Sometimes, people made their own caves by digging spaces in the sides of cliffs.

Today, few people live in caves. Some modern-day cave homes are dug out of mine tunnels, cliffs or natural caves. Cave homes use less energy than other homes. In hot regions, cave homes stay cool naturally. These homes usually have furniture, plumbing and a power source.

Caves are exciting places to explore. They are filled with interesting features and are among the most incredible places on Earth.

Predjama Castle was built into a cliff in front of a cave in Slovenia. It is the largest cave castle in the world.

Glossary

artefacts *(noun)*	objects made by human beings
bacteria *(noun)*	single-celled organisms found on living and non-living things
caches *(noun)*	stores of things hidden away
calcium *(noun)*	a soft white substance found in plants and animals
crevasses *(noun)*	deep cracks in a glacier
decorations *(noun)*	features that look interesting or attractive
dissolves *(verb)*	mixes with a liquid and disappears
evaporates *(verb)*	turns from liquid into vapour
hazards *(noun)*	objects or actions that can be dangerous
hoard *(noun)*	a store of objects, usually kept secret or hidden
mineral *(noun)*	a substance that is formed naturally in rocks
molten *(adjective)*	heated to a high temperature and become a thick liquid
preserve *(verb)*	to look after something well; keep in its original condition
silhouettes *(noun)*	drawings of the outline of something
speleologists *(noun)*	scientists who study caves
spelunkers *(noun)*	another word for cavers, or people who explore caves for fun
twilight *(noun)*	the time after sunset when it is just getting dark

Index